Schoolyard Crushes

&

Prozac Prescriptions

Poems by

Tori Lutz

2021

For Peter

Schoolyard Crushes

&

Prozac Prescriptions

CONTENTS

Introduction

So much of our emotional development in the most formative years of our lives can be tied to the little moments that make up the biggest pictures. First loves, first losses, first clumsy and painful navigations through our own mental health. Many of the most passionate and striking memories can be found in these 'firsts' that have brought us to new chapters in life.

This book is about those firsts as well as the roads they can lead down. It captures both the giddy joy of new experiences as well as the jaded retrospection of an older self. We may no longer be our innocent childhood selves, but the stories from that era in our lives became the clay that molded who we are now.

From my first kiss to my first mental health prescription, I have grown and changed and lived so much. This is my attempt at a love letter to all of those beautiful moments that made themselves a part of the mosaic I now see in the mirror. After all, some of the shiniest things are made up of little broken fragments.

I hope this collection speaks to all of your glittering pieces as well. May the picture they create give everything you've carried a purpose.

"Come back to the city it was easiest for you to breathe in."

- Blythe Baird

BUT FIRST, A DISCLAIMER:

Mi vida –
I've never been good at letting go.
If I were to touch poison ivy,
I wouldn't snap my
hand back
and
scramble to heal
the burn. I'd sit among
the weeds and wrap myself in
a blanket of stinging stars. I'd fall
asleep not even recognizing
the itch as something
wrong because
at least
it's familiar. At
least it's a pain I can
recognize, can sleep off, can
pretend is all in my head like everything
else.

EVEN GOOD STORIES END

I spend the seasons we're speaking
believing you to be little more
than a band-aid, yet every
other chapter of my life seems
to be nothing more than a bookmark
between pages softened by the oils
of your fingertips.
I loved you before I understood
why I wanted to hold your hand,
before you realized why you
always seemed to notice when I
wasn't in the room.

The eras between You are parallel
to the worlds built with my nose
in a book.
        Striking.
                Developmental.

    New.

But every time I lift my head up
again, every time another story
comes to an end, I look up
            and
               find
                  you.

SUFFOCATING

Breathe in.
Breathe out.

ON A SCALE OF 1-10 HOW ARE YOU FEELING
TODAY?

One meaning one foot
in the grave
and the other barely grabbing the edge

Ten meaning tenacious,
vivacious,
and every other
acious
that can describe how
elated you are.

MAYBE YOU'RE FEELING A FIVE IF YOU'RE JUST
DOING FINE.

There is no right answer. Of course,
unless
you consider
anything
below a four
the right
answer.

Four because we care for
you
and can't let anything bad
happen.

SO LET'S LOCK THAT SHIT DOWN BEFORE IT
BECOMES A PROBLEM.

Because we can't have you
                    I mean you
                              I mean
          YOUR
                    BRAIN
     SHUTTING DOWN
                         ON US NOW

But answer honestly.

ON A SCALE OF 1-10 HOW ARE YOU FEELING
TODAY?

No pressure but
                    you aren't the
          only one
                    with *problems*
and we need to know how
          ~~serious~~
this is before we can
                    move on.

                              MOVE ON.

Can you say at least a six?

          Sorry?

                    Sick of this,
          no,
                    at least a six.

I'LL JUST JOT DOWN SEVEN IF IT'S ALL THE SAME
TO YOU THEN.

You look ^{chipper} enough today,

                         keep

                       that   *up!*

                             head

We all know what happened
    when you last reached
        a two, a two as in
Too

      Fucking

           Bad

You've got **shit** to do.

I think we should aim for
            an eight by tomorrow
if you ate before tomorrow
      we could even put a
NINE.

But I'm not sure you're there yet and it's
      asinine to shoot too high so
HOW ABOUT THAT SEVEN AGAIN?

What?

    Three?

THAT WON'T DO YOU SEE

That has to be documented
          prioritized
             considered a
          problem
             other people
          have real problems.

CAN'T YOU SEE WE DON'T HAVE TIME FOR A
CRISIS?

If you're gonna fuck up

> *at least*

>> *do it*

>>> *right.*

> ~~*Breathe in.*~~

~~*Breathe out.*~~

LOVE IN CURSIVE

They say
"Don't bring a knife to a gunfight."
But I think my problem
is bringing love letters
to a knife fight. And the knives
always end up
deep
in my back
before I can even
get past the first
few lines,
choking and gargling
a perverted variation of
what those pages were
supposed to be,

crumpled up and torn now
in the pockets of my
jeans. I wonder
what a full
letter
would sound like
out loud.

Would it sound like
the stained-glass cage
around my heart
shattering
into a million
little
pieces,
grinding

into a fine kaleidoscope
of dust?

Maybe that's just me
romanticizing
another
missed
opportunity.

HEART-SHAPED STONES IN YOUR BACKPACK

It is okay to mourn what you've given away

     even if you have no regrets about the separation.

No one tells you that being born to love

     is the most unearned and heartbreaking burden

the Earth can bless you with.

     Love anyway.

CALL IT WHAT YOU WANT

To believe in a soulmate
         is an arrogant thing –
                  it is to believe that
         you are as perfect for
someone as it can get, as
         perfect for them as you
                  know they are for
         you.
Can you instead sit with
         me, then, at the top of
                  the double slide? I
         can tell you secrets that
I pinky promise I've never
         told anyone else before.
                  That I don't want to go
         home.

                  That I like you.

         That I want you.

                  That I love you.

That I need you.

That however I gravitate
         toward or away from
                  you is instinct that
         can't be explained by
the words and languages
         I have spent the better

half of my life mastering,
loving.
Maybe that's why you were
always the first person I'd
look for in hide-and-seek.
Maybe that's why we
seem to spend the intersections
of our lives still playing even
after everyone else has gone
home.

THAT BITCH NEXT DOOR

She's a *bitch.*

She envelopes you like humidity,
calls you at 2
                3
                    4 am
                    till you abandon sleep completely,
dictates when you can do anything that makes you happy.

She takes you and
                            breaks you and
                                            makes you
                        into f_r^ag_m^en_ts of yourself
that are too sharp to put back together
but too dull to make anything worthwhile.

She locks you in your room regardless of your plans,
slowly closes
                    around your neck with her cold,
            bare hands
and you will be *damned* before she begins to let go.

She plucks your   out of your life,
                        loved ones
demands 100% of your undivided attention
and bleeds your every emotion
bone
dry.

After a while, her name will be etched into your skin,
marking her territory and reminding you that she *owns you.*

                                        Knows you.
                        Chose you.

Her stopwatch can freeze your life –
        dissolve the future, warp the past –
make seconds feel like years
                        and years feel like ^mountains
                you were never meant to cli^mb

And she's always armed and ready when things fall apart
        as she innocently numbs your ~~pain~~
                until your ~~emotions~~ evaporate
        completely before your eyes
and leave you holding on
                                to nothing
                but the air
                        that has become too **thick** to
        breathe.

She contorts your passions into nuisances
        with an artful subtly that makes it seem like
Your Own Belief™

She holds you with a comforting familiarity
        that *almost* makes you scared to let her leave
and **oh**,
        you can *try* to make her leave,
make her stop **knocking**
                        and **talking**
                        and **prodding**,
erase her voice from your memory
and her fingerprints from your heart,

13

but you can't put band-aids on a geyser
and think it'll be ~~silenced.~~
        You can't beat down a monster
That doesn't ~~bleed.~~
        You can't fight her off without
                        fighting yourself
because her permanent address is
                                inside
                                        your
                                                head.

Depression is a **bitch**
                and she doesn't give a damn
        who thinks so.

INSTAGRAM REELS & REAL WORLD FEELS

Here's a smiling selfie I took on this beautiful day!
> *This is one of 23 photos I took and didn't throw away.*

My food is so delicious, and this lighting is so pretty!
> *I barely took a bite and a half and I already feel guilty.*

I miss this girl so much!! #BFF #WCW #WCE my love!
> *I haven't left my house or made new friends in months.*

My latest graduation cap is a stunning shade of blue!
> *I'm another $80,000 in debt without a job or a clue.*

Just a glass of wine or two after an exhausting week!
> *I spent most of it in bed and the bottle will be empty.*

#TBT back when I was the world's silliest baby!
> *I don't remember the last time I felt this purely happy.*

Finally got some sand between my toes and fun in the sun!
> *I spent $150 on this bikini and don't hate how I look for once.*

I'm going offline for a bit for a chance to focus on me!
> *I'm exhausted by this app and begging for a moment to breathe.*

BEDTIME STORIES

You'd think that all the repeat dreams I dream
would be enough to let me go to sleep.

I

Little me always
loved the mystery
of music boxes.

Guarded by a melody,
shielding secrets, tempting
me like Pandora. Only a latch
between me and everything
I've yet to see.

The box the boy handed
little me was tragically
beautiful
and heavy. I still sleep
with it every night,
long after I flooded

my unknowing world
with secrets that I doubt
even Pandora was permitted
to know about. I think

I understand her
overwhelming curiosity.
Except Pandora
had a warning.

II

Hunger made more sense
before changing her name
to Loneliness.

Eating made more sense
when it was designed
to nurture, not to linger.

It's hard to miss sunshine
when I feel warmest covered
in his flames, hard to
remember moderation
when I'm drunk
on the toughest games.

Persephone swore she only took
six seeds or twenty-six weeks
but I'm still wiping the juice
off my chin from swallowing
the whole thing.

III

The final acts
in fairytales
are never what
we are set up
to anticipate.

They leave us hungrier
and emptier and quieter
than the opening pages,
using potential closure
to kindle the fire.

I haunt the middles
of the stories for as long
as I can manage but

I can't avoid the ending
where Peter
loses Wendy;
why do anxiety
and falling in love
feel inseparably alike?

You'd think that all the repeat dreams I dream
would be enough to let me go to sleep.

CUL-DE-SAC
a villanelle

With lessons learned on roads that never end,
I'm sure I've seen all I can see until
I've lost my equilibrium again.

I learned to ride my bike when I was ten.
The cul-de-sac would test my grit and will
With lessons learned on roads that never end.

I gave my youth to feel what "love" had meant.
Although I'd say the ache was worth the thrill,
I've lost my equilibrium again.

The pains that come with growing up don't mend.
This child has learned to fight, to hide, to kill,
With lessons learned on roads that never end.

I've sat and cried outside a CVS.
They had no script to get my pills refilled;
I've lost my equilibrium again.

And so it seems that just around the bend
Will always be a way to take a spill.
With lessons learned on roads that never end,
I've lost my equilibrium again.

GOLD EXCHANGED FOR LIQUID COPPER

If I pulled my childhood self aside
and told her that one day
we'd be able to inhale silver,
swallow copper, turn golden
moments into misty memories
that almost erase
               the mistakes –
would she believe in magic?
After all, how many witches
and warlocks, heroes and
heroines have exchanged their
happiness|family|dreams|love|future|lives
for their power?

And isn't this like
       its own form
              of immortality
     after all?

I wouldn't call it decay –

The worms won't even want me;
I taste too bitter.

I guess even if you get the recipe
perfect, you'll still end up with
sour cake if you use spoiled
ingredients.

But how could such glittering
    things be rotten?

Silver and gold racing down my throat
filling my chest, my abdomen,

my vat of promises that
I'll figure it out
> *I'll figure it out*
>> *I'll figure out*
> *I'm fine*
I'm fine

I'M FINE.

Turns out that if I get as wasted
as my potential,

I don't care.
I feel good.

THE NIGHT I ALMOST RUINED A LIFE

i coated my throat in irish whiskey to prove i could keep up
with the boys. the two of us were drinking like hemingway
– real writers – last one still sober wins. last one still standing
wins. last one with a hope of a memory of the entire ordeal
gets the trophy. secretly i knew i didn't want to win. i love
winning but i love forgetting more. slicing my thoughts into
ice cubes to fill my glass. washing it down with swigs
straight from the bottle. poor john doe had to deal with me.
poor john doe had to lift me onto his bed. poor john doe had
to remind me of everything that just happened and brew me
tea. had to chase me half-naked around the parking lot until
i realized i had nowhere to go and came back inside. leant
me a book to pretend to read. gave me a pen to write my
damn self a letter. didn't sleep until 5 a.m. almost had his
life ruined when i pondered telling anyone anything i
remembered or imagined – his hand on my thigh his fists
around my arms his sweat on my skin – maybe that's why i
still can't say his name. maybe that's why i couldn't ruin his
life back. i hope the next girl is less forgiving. i hope she
shows her teeth and is out for blood, his blood, blood to refill
her own veins and use as ink for his sentencing. i hope john
doe will never be the same. i hope he will never forget her
like he did me.

THE MIRACLE DIET

I often picture myself physically withering
away, one particle at a time, until I am
nothing more than a gossamer in
the shape of a girl who used to
dance, the promises my life
used to give me, the web
of potential that's since
been cleared away by
the absentminded
flick of a feather
duster I used to
own. Until I am
nothing but a
death rattle,
a final
sigh
of
re
li
e
f

QUICK GLANCE AT MY GOOGLE SEARCH HISTORY

Are geckos sentient
Best dandruff shampoo
When was the accordion invented
How long does arsenic take
Rehab near me
Abnormal pap smear meaning
Cervical cancer survival rates
Spanish to English
Flights to Miami
Waxing near me
COVID-19 cases NYC
New York unemployment
Taylor Swift net worth
Tattoo shops near me
Best tattoo concealer
Tori Lutz
Calories in a strawberry
Tarantula hawk wasp
Why do flies like poop so much
Why do flies like dead bodies so much
Least painful ways to die
Least painful ways to almost die
If I die will my cat eat me
Why do cats eat the eyeballs first
How much is lasik
Are my boobs normal
Why is life so long
Why is life so short
How do cockroaches live without heads
How to be as tough as a cockroach

Quarter life crisis
Can I swim across the Atlantic ocean
Synonyms for heartbroken
Why does love make you crazy
Why does crying make you blotchy
Why does Prozac make me shake
Why does mental illness exist
Why does God never answer in complete sentences
How can I stop feeling so sad
How can I stop feeling
How can I just go the fuck to sleep

I NEVER DID GROW FOND OF SHOELACES

which
may be why the
wet chill of fresh snow
or grime from high-traffic
streets never did agree with me.
The city stains on my naked, pale
feet are proof that I'm too hard-headed
hard-footed or just too damned hard to
flipflops away. My nails aren't painted
stick out, but these shoes are on and off
They're the staple of the Beach Bum's
of anyone ready to fling them off with
in the street / sand / puddles/ any-and-
accept footprints as a valid form of
statue placed in the wrong exhibit
shoes press in on me like I've just
dignified at all costs. I just can't
Both. I'm tired of all the trendy
to give or take a goddamn thing
yes, that's a lot of pressure to
my sandcastles will always be
these years suffocating the crap
I just can't take the aches and
might be time. I think home is
paycheck will come from, more
Instagram Post, more than cool
with hip themes that make no
breathe, where you can rest
be your most honest self.
can't stop thinking
something

or
throw my
and my callouses do
faster than I could ask of them.
uniform, the sleek glass slipper
one kick so they can dance barefoot
everywhere they go. Places that don't
currency make my body feel more like a
or a fat tourist in my own skin. Closed toe
signed a contract to remain covered, clean,
breathe in there/I mean those/I mean both?
shoes-people-places that never want you
and just sit down, sit pretty, sit still and
place on lazy footwear but hell, even
dramatic. The Big City™ has spent
out of me/I mean my feet and Lord
blisters anymore. Mama, I think it
more than where the next big girl
than the place that makes the Best
friends or *sexy* strangers in the bars
*** sense. Home is where you can
with real peace and know you can
Home is with the person you just
about without feeling like there's
missing from your day. I promise
I am grateful that I learned what
else is out there, but I think the
biggest lesson was on how
to draw out a roadmap
to lead me back
Home.

IF HALLMARK MADE A CARD FOR EVERYTHING

how many puns could they make
out of sorry-about-your-colonoscopy?
How many cardboard castles
might be dedicated to sweet romantic
musings for the Side Chick on Valentine's Day™?

What colors would they use to capture
a sorry-your-parents-sold-your-childhood-home
condolence card? I bet they'd have a hell
of a time figuring out the details for a
congrats-on-losing-your-virginity pop-up

(or perhaps something more along the
lines of a sorry-I-came-in-seventeen-seconds
IOU would be a more likely bestseller). I
doubt I speak for just myself when I say
I'd be browsing the fuck-that-guy-girlfriend cards.

If the aisles went on forever and the
cardstock depicted every godforsaken
human emotion/experience/wish/mistake,
what sentiments might overflow my mailbox
and what cheesy one-liners would I

feel compelled to stuff into crinkly
envelopes? Maybe if everything came
on an overpriced compulsory gesture,
we'd have fewer question marks and more
how-the-fuck-did-you-find-a-card-for-my-

eating-disorder-what-drawer-does-this-
even-get-stuffed-into-GOD-can't-Hallmark-
go-back-to-making-fucking-movies-instead-
I-thought-they-profited-off-people's-innate-
horror-at-being-honest.

DRUNK IN MY KITCHEN'S CHURCH

I don't remember how you got stuck in my throat.

No, this isn't another sexy poem
No, this isn't another trauma poem
This, my darling, is my
          e x h a u s t i o n
at gargling my own heartbeat.
This, my love, is my **FRUSTRATION**
at counting bees in my veins
as I try to
calm down
          c a l m   d o w n
                    C A L M

This, my dear, mi vida, is my [plea]
for release
from the
C H O K E H O L D
of my own   nonsense

And it's funny!
Because anyone who is also fed
                              up
with this barbed wire sweater
has known since about
f
i
v
e
seconds in
what this concoction of ramblings and
cacophony of

nOnSenSiCaL characters
is about.

Y E S –
my lover, my steadfast anxiety.

And oh, I'd have loved
to maintain ambiguity,
to maintain the cloak
of imagery, of metaphor, of
a bs tra c t
that would turn this
into an artful piece of *writing*
instead of an on-the-nose
cry for

HELP.

But I think
I cut off my nose
to spite the mind
behind
it
a long time ago, if you get me,
and I'm just tired now.

Sana, sana, colita de rana
doesn't work for everything.

I'm tired of choking on wine
to stop *h y p e r v e n t a l a t i n g*
- to give myself a tangible problem
to deal with
so I don't stay
doggy paddling up shit's creek.

Yes, it's okay if you laughed
at that image, it's fucking funny.

But yes, it's also okay if you
frowned, if you're
wondering why I'm not committed,
if you're stuck between
PITY | AND | HORROR
with no idea where the scale is
supposed to balance out.

Because I am constantly
all of those things at once
when I'm in this poem,
when I'm dancing with the words
on the page, trying to make them
love me,
trying to make them
my friend,
to make them more than
worn-out life vests
that squeeze a little too tight on some days
and don't even inflate at all on others.

It's either this or splashing sour red wine
on white countertops, ruining
an innocent blood orange
that was in the way.

And it was only kind of worth it –
the wine is shit, it tastes like
communion.

But maybe that's a good way
to keep me from overfilling
the glass again.

I wish I could tell you that this poem was
drunk –
that it SPLASHED out of me that it was
s p a c e d
                    o u t
or high or driven by some force
that wasn't my own

because honestly
it's EMBARRASSING
that this is the most
coherent stream
I've *stitched* together
in about
a *YEAR.*

And I thought that was the inspiration
people moved to New York to find.

God, I hope you think I'm crazy
because at least I'll know you think of me.

I MISS THE BLISTERS ON MY FEET

I used to walk
barefoot
to your house.
I was 14 and dirt
didn't bother me.
The crunch of leaves

and texture of grass
and sidewalk cracks were
worth calloused toes.

It's rare for me
to leave my shoes
behind nowadays.

After all, the cold
ground prickles my
feet now since

I left the sun
back with you
in my hometown

and my body knows
that this time,
I'm not walking to you.

ASTRONOMY LESSONS

I am so sorry
it took me so long
to realize you could
love me in more
than the abstract.
I've been grasping at
stars and constellations
that have long since burned
out while you have been
waiting to fill my ribcage
with entire galaxies.

Please forgive me
for being too starstruck
to let you hold me.

MIND RACERS

You don't live in my mind,
but you have a habit of strolling
        through it, perusing as if
exploring an abandoned mall
                from your childhood.
        I see you

                every few

                        months or so.

Does someone beautiful rest
next to you at night?

                        Did you finish those
                        degrees, dreams, destinies?

Do I ever find my way into
the curves of your thoughts?

                        Or did you figure out
                        how to change the locks?

Have you changed the world
yet like you've changed mine?

                        Did leaving our neighborhood
                        burn the bridges behind you?

I thought it did
for me when I left.

I hope at the end
of the day, you'll
keep at least one
candle lit in the window

in case I come

Home.

CHILD IN ME

I'm stronger
than the little
girl who was
scared to admit
she liked you,

who asked her
diary when she
might get her
first kiss and
what the tingles

meant. I'm older
than the child
who fell for
everything that
tasted sweet,

who may have
danced awkwardly
but also danced
passionately when
you weren't looking.

But I hope you
still see her
sparkle in my
eyes if you
look closely.

RESURRECTING RUINS

Bruising my knees hits differently
on crooked cobblestones that once
led
            the way
                        home.
I think it was a lifetime
and a half ago that the road was

                                    smooth
                        dependable
                                    free
            of bloodstains and bad
                                    memories.
I wish I could have shown it to you

                        then,

the smoking gray stones gently strangled
            by ivy
                        and lavender
                                    and the twinkling
                        dust
                                    I've crafted my
            heart from.

I feel like you might've wanted to memorize
it then. Understand the
                        gentle curves and
            scenic backdrops –
but all that I can offer now are
                                    plunging cliffs and
                        poisoned forests.

But I

         will

                try.

I will bruise and bloody my hands and knees
    until the deep sanguine smudges
       wash the grime
           and fill the cracks
and I can lead you down a road
         worth
           following.

LITTLEST SURPRISES

You were the prom dress
I fell in love with.
You hugged my curves
and held my eyes,

pushed me out of my
comfort zone in the best ways.

And I didn't even notice
until I took you home

and tried you on in my
own mirror in my own room

that you have pockets
on top of it all.

I DROWN IN MY OWN SPOTLIGHT

I can see myself in all I experience:
the protagonist of my own story,
the self-absorbed anxiety that rests
underneath the placid waters
of my humility.
When I see a swallow
I don't see a bird,
I see my panicked,
scrambled,
oh-shit-I-set-my-alarm-for-PM
weekday pandemonium. I see
the harmony to my
morning coffee.

When I see a pen
I don't see stationery,
I see my sword, my
lifeline, my claim
to fame
and the tool
behind my own
signature.

When I see you with her
I don't see a love story.
I see my own reflection
scattered among the
shards and dust
of a shattering
mirror.

DEPRESS-IPES

I. Toast
    1. Sniff a stiff slice of bread
    2. Check for blue fuzz
    3. Shove it in the toaster
    4. Pray it doesn't burn

II. Ramen and Iced Coffee
    1. Chuck the noodles in boiling water
    2. Overpay for an app to deliver one coffee you won't finish
    3. Burn your tongue on the ramen so you can't taste that you forgot the seasoning
    4. Defy all odds and take a caffeine-loaded nap
    Tip: Don't open the blinds to spoil the is-this-breakfast-lunch-or-dinner surprise!

III. The Inside of Your Cheek
    1. Find something of insurmountable stress or inconvenience
    2. Chew

IV. Toast
    1. You know what to do

V. The skin peeling from picked lips
    1. Lick off the layer of medicinal ChapStick
    2. Don't forget the rusty seasoning that tastes like pennies
    2. Reseal leftovers with another coat of ChapStick

VI. ???
   1. Pull shit out from the back of the pantry
   2. Hope for the best

VII. Jungle Juice
   1. Find a bottle
   2. Find a glass
   3. Go nuts

VIII. Tub O' Ice Cream
   1. Match a flavor to your self-pity movie of choice
   2. Run a large spoon under warm water for easy
       scooping
   3. Try not to puke halfway through the carton

IX. Water
   1. Hell yeah
   2. You did it
   3. Self-care
   4. Now reward yourself with a 5-hour nap

X. Crackers, Applesauce, and the Holy Bible
   1. Eat slowly so your body doesn't realize what's
       happening
   2. Keep the applesauce close by whenever an
       appetite arrives
   3. Pray that tomorrow will be a clearer day

DON'T TWEET YOUR HEROES

Or if you do / make sure you're drunk / or stoned / or a little bit of both / because heroes are bones / and bones / build palaces / become foundations / of belief systems / of dreams / of expectations / but give them the chance / to supply their own / sticks and stones / and I promise they will / never be the weapons you / expected / God knows / they'll never stick around / long enough to save you / to live up to the benefit / of your doubt / God knows that at the end / of the day / heroes are humans too / heroes are failures too / heroes might as well be / you

EVERGREEN

You never forget
or lose your   grip
on your first love. It's life's
purest connection, the smell
of smoke that takes you
          from childhood
to fairytale
          to loss
and back again
with something as mundane
as a polaroid,
               a yearbook,
a pressed flower
          from a corsage
that's long since
               wilted.

DO FISH MISS THEIR PONDS?

My world used to be the size
of a zip code. Three blocks
from the love of my life
that slipped through my fingers
every winter like a gasp,
five blocks from the only
friend, only soul who has loved
me through every one of my
worsts – yes, even
that one – a mile

away from my favorite
bookstore, from the school
that grew me, from the
now gone tea shop that warmed
my throat and kept my books

company. It's hard to find all
of this when borders are
destroyed and my world
feels boundless. Cities are cold
but some things are bound to bounce

back.

WISHING I HAD THE MIND TO LOVE YOU

I tossed my life savings
in the form of countless
pennies into a bottomless
well.
No refunds.

        No returns.

            No exchanges.

I'm still waiting
to hear
the splash.

PERFECT TIMING WITH A BROKEN WATCH

I wonder what would happen
if we missed each other
at the same time.
Would the universe flip inside
out, rewriting Destiny's entire
playbook, just so we could
bump into each other?

If we loved each other
at the same time, would
all the particles in the
galaxy finally buzz
in harmony?

Would the Earth stop
turning for a fraction
of a second like the jolt
of a missed heartbeat?

Would time freeze?
        Would the dust settle?
Would everyone else's face
        blur over for just a moment?

Like the first time
                        you kissed me?

Maybe.

BIRTHDAY CAKE FROSTING

I always save one candle on my birthday cake
        to wish on you.

I almost don't even want
        to set it ablaze, but
                when has it ever
        been less than a
forest fire with you?

I secretly hope that the too-sweet frosting
        will give me a cavity
                that will taste like
        you,

taste like the candy in your voice
        that's given me such
                a sweet tooth.

I leave a chair empty even at the most crowded
        party,

even if a dozen people are left standing
        because I'm secretly
                hoping it'll be filled by
        you.

I'm not supposed to tell anyone my wish
        but if I spill it to you,
                will you show?

I turn up the volume on my phone
        so I won't miss the ghost of a
            phone call

        just in case
you finally decide
        to haunt me
                outside my dreams
        this year.

That's the thing about hope, isn't it?
        You can never really talk yourself
out of it.

CRACKED GLASS CONFESSIONS

Telling you everything wrong with me
felt like a death sentence, the last
amount of pressure that would
shatter the fishbowl and flood
the house with poison that would
never fit inside a container again.
Every atom in my body was sure
you would choke on my alphabet
soup of Fucked Up. That you would
curse my name with your last breaths
of innocence, of normalcy, of peace.
I mourned you before I even finished

the sentence. And yet, you're here.
You're breathing. You're placing
that fishbowl on a higher shelf
to keep it safe and to keep
me dry.

PHANTOM IN A BOTTLE

I hope you can't taste
the ghost of whisky
in the back of my throat
when you kiss me.
I followed my fears
to the bottom
of the bottle
and it led me
here,

showing you my worst,
my most bitter, most
pathological.

I don't know if a clear head
and a quiet heart
would have emptied this
out of me like the contents
of a hope chest

and I don't know how you still
look at me like that, like I'm
brave, like I'm
good.

Maybe you're a little wasted too.

PSYCH WARD SOCKS

You have a better grip on anything
than I ever will. Pale blue
like my eyes yet calmer, soothing
and smoothing even the toughest wrinkles.
You're my quietest trophy, proof
that my pain is certifiable *and* survivable.
Everyone who also knows will recognize you
and the rest linger on you the same
as any sock; the ones with the tacos
are cuter anyway. But you, you don't
need the flair, the distractions. You're the opposite,
steadfast and solid and one of the only
pairs with whom I could never part.
Those stuck-up taco socks could never
make me smile through the tears like you.
They could never stay soft through
special-occasion-only use. Thank you for
your service as a souvenir on my worst days.
Thank you for keeping me warm
through a different kind of cold.
I don't always remember the cacophony
of thoughts/fears/unmentionables that sent me to the E.R.
that night, that left me catatonic and my
mother terrified. But you, I know you.
You are a permanent staple in my wardrobe
even if you'll never be worn from use.
Thank you for being the uniform
of a night I survived without knowing I would.

LOVE LETTERS AND PHARMACISTS

I noticed that the sun
on my skin today
      felt more like a
hug than a
            burn,
noticed my coffee
had flavor,
      my footsteps
felt lighter,
         my voice
      didn't scrape
through my throat.

Maybe it's the ~~10~~
            ~~20~~
    ~~40~~

        80 milligrams
swimming through my veins
      on any given day.
Maybe it's the way
      the labyrinths of your
    fingertips press into
mine to remind
    me
      I'll be okay.

THE ART OF KEEPING YOU WARM

I've been on one
         of my lowest streaks
but if you implied
         that you needed me
to get my *shit*
         together, I'd light
myself on fire
         and shine bright
enough to guide
         you back home.

IS THERE RUST IN YOUR ARMOR?

What makes your heart s t u t t e r
      like it only has a single moment
to proclaim its truth
              or burst into flames?
What makes your stomach twist
beneath your *rough*,
           unscratched
surface? When have you been
      nervous to
speak or
      slow to
sleep?

Have you ever looked at
      me and felt like your ribcage
might crack under the pressure
      of your held breath?

I wish
      I could read
            your eyes
      like the books
that
      litter my
            apartment
      floor.

Maybe
      I'd see myself.
Maybe
      I make you a little nervous
too.

ANSWERING ECHOES
a pantoum

Do your ears ring when I write about you?
My pens are running out of ink.
Another sun has gone down.
I soak my tongue in sour wine.

My pens are running out of ink.
My desk is covered in crumpled pages.
I soak my tongue in sour wine.
Maybe it'll look different in morning light.

My desk is covered in crumpled pages.
Poetic origami.
Maybe it'll look different in morning light.
Maybe one more glass will make it right.

Poetic origami.
My words are tumbling in a foreign tongue.
Maybe one more glass will make it right.
Do your drinks whisper about me too?

My words are tumbling in a foreign tongue.
Another sun has gone down.
Do your drinks whisper about me too?
Do your ears ring when I write about you?

I SWORE I'D NEVER WRITE LOVE POEMS

before you managed to make it my vocation,
my area of expertise devoted
to an expert tease.
before I knew eyes could look like yours,
could make blinking feel like forever
with how much I miss seeing them
in those sliced seconds.

before I knew that your hand
on the small of my back
would feel like the same
warm velvet as rum
swimming through
my body.

before you showed me
that love and poetry
cannot exist separately.

Am I a poet yet?

REDEFINING SPECIAL

You don't look at me
like I'm the only girl
in the world.
You look at me like
you've **met** every girl
and know for a fact

that I'm the one
you want to spend
twenty lifetimes loving.

THE ONE THAT GOT ~~AWAY~~ ~~AWAY~~ AWAY?

I bet the pennies I've tossed
wishing for you could have
paid for my ticket out of here,
could have paid for this most
recent effort to come home.
They say the most fleeting
moments are the ones

you'll find flashing before your
eyes when the car swerves too
quickly, when the pavement
rushes too eagerly, when you
ache to exist in any moment
but the one you're in.

God knows why.

It's easier to catch the smoke
from your cigarette with bare,
shaky fingers than to keep
hold of your hand but that
has never seemed to stop
me from grasping.
I wish we used our ebb
and flow for dancing instead
taking turns loving each other –
heart-shaped satellites in the night – and
pretending it doesn't hurt.

If you saw my face when I stepped on the plane,
maybe this time I wouldn't have gotten away.

BEING CHOKED WITH A SMILE

The salt
on your lips
tastes like the
ocean that
will drown
me.
Holding
my breaths
safe inside my
chest has
never
felt

this
good.

THE FACE OF THE CLOCK AT 4 A.M.

looks a lot like yours if I squint hard enough,
a lot like the mouth that swallowed me up
with the promise of just one kiss.

No wonder we burrow into separate corners
of the Earth to avoid talking about it –

Honesty can taste like bottom-of-the-pantry 151
but we sure do love our sticky bottles
and cracked glass. God knows
I don't need a litmus test for the acidity
      in your voice.

At least, that's how I like to remember it;
it makes it easier to swallow than just
considering you gone. You know how
I am with simpler truths.

The tequila shoots down smooth
      but I choke on the lime
every time.

I miss playing drinking games
      with shots of apple cider
         and pretending to be
    grown.

Maybe next time you take me out
      we can get apple juice instead.

I wish I could have seen
        the beauty
        in things like that.

I grew up in paradise and I fled it –
        back when I thought
chasing my dreams
        and coming back home
were mutually exclusive
        realities.

MAGNUM OPUS

Your place in my life
is a masterpiece in
the making.
       My longest devotion.
             My most complex line work.
                   My lifetime of achievement.

I'd never use an eraser –
not even when it blurs
not even when it gets dirty –
the smudges tie it
together best.

       My one request,
            my only price tag,
                my only exchange

is that whatever
the finished product may
be, you hang it proudly.

       My biggest mistakes.
          My shining moments.
             My voice every time I say your
name.

Immortalize all of it
so that the artist may
be appreciated in her time.

PRETTY PILLS

If love could be measured
in milligrams, I'd overdose
on you.
Pack you into my Pez Dispenser
and make a coma taste
like candy.
You're the kind of medicine
that doesn't need a
chaser,
the kind of danger
that leaves the good type of burn
in my throat, chest, stomach
and feels better
than healing.

If only you weren't so damn
pretty, maybe then I'd read the
directions, the warning
label.
Maybe then I'd remember I'm not
choking on SweeTarts as my eyes
flutter shut.

DRESS REHEARSALS

A disastrous run-through
         means a beautiful opening night,

         right?

So we tore the costumes
         to shreds
and knocked down all
         of the sets.
So we crumpled up
         the scripts
and smashed the stage
         lights in.

So we set
                  the theater
                           blazing.

We can still waltz
         until the curtain
                  signals
         our final
bow.

"So we beat on, boats against the current, as we are borne back ceaselessly into the past."

- F. Scott Fitzgerald

Acknowledgments

There are so many beautiful and loving people who made this collection a reality. I couldn't possibly thank every soul who has helped me on this journey but know that I am forever grateful for you regardless.

To my dear readers for taking the chance to support a budding author and listen to my stories.

To my incredible parents and family, thank you for supporting the writer in me my entire life. You gave me the tools, the resources, and the support to do it all.

To my mentor, Cameron Hawkins, for taking a shy poet and turning her into a performer and an artist. I also want to thank Nick Austin, Johnathan Riley, and everyone else in Poetic Lyricism for reading my roughest drafts and making me the writer and person I am today.

To my grade-school teachers Kearon Bird and Laura Yusko. The way you nourished my love for books and read all of my silly songs and stories helped me realize how deep my passion runs and all I can do with it.

To my university professors Barbara Hamby, David Kirby, Jimmy Kimbrel, and Celia Caputi who oversaw my thesis as I put together my first collection of poetry. You taught me everything that I'm proud of as a poet.

To the impossibly talented Sabrina Benaim, taking your course has truly helped my poetry to evolve to the next level. You are truly an inspiration; never stop teaching and never stop writing.

To Jess Beasley and all the hours we have spent in libraries and coffee shops to make the dream happen. There is no one I'd rather grind away through dozens of poems with.

To Sarah Goldberg for being a constant poet companion and always reading my first drafts. You remind me every day that poetry is the true love of my life.

To Tee Hamilton, the brightest source of creativity my life has ever known. I miss you every single day.

To Kelly McKenna for standing by my side and cheering me on before I ever showed promise. You have supported every dream of mine and I am so blessed to have known you.

To Madeleine, Hanna, Heath, Lia, Rebecca, Shelby, Nicky, Wes, and every single one of my friends who have made such an incredible support system and inspiration. You've loved me through my demons and diagnoses, and I wouldn't be here without you.

And, of course, Peter, for giving me books of stories to tell over the years. Thank you for making a big city feel smaller and small dreams feel like oceans.

About the Author

Tori is a poet from Miami, Florida. She received a Bachelor of Arts in English from Florida State University (2018) and a Master of Science in Journalism from Columbia University (2021). She is currently living in New York City pursuing journalism and poetry.

Her love of writing began with her love of reading when she discovered the *Harry Potter* series at the age of six. Since then, she has explored songwriting, short and long fiction, non-fiction, poetry, and academic writing.

With a persistent passion in English, Tori studied Creative Writing at Florida State University from 2014-2018. Here she discovered the organization Poetic Lyricism which is responsible for who she is as an artist to this day. She also discovered the student newspaper, the FSView & Florida Flambeau, where she learned to combine her love of writing with her ambition and work ethic.

She also completed an Honors Thesis at Florida State University that comprised of 75 pages of original poetry. This collection, titled *Letters to Lilith*, is currently in the works to be expanded and perfected as an official book release.

https://www.torilutzpoetry.com
Instagram: @torilutzpoetry
This is her first collection of poetry.